This book is for you

IF

you are a parent, be it
married,
single,
step,
working;

AND

you sincerely want to understand
why your adolescent is behaving
the way he or she does;

AND

you want to learn effective
ways to respond to and successfully
cope with that behavior.

Coping with your Adolescent

Larry Waldman, Ph.D.

HAMPTON ROADS
PUBLISHING COMPANY, INC.

Cover design by Patrick Smith

For information write:

Hampton Roads Publishing Company, Inc.
891 Norfolk Square
Norfolk, VA 23502

Or call: (804)459-2453
FAX: (804)455-8907

If you are unable to order this book from your local
bookseller, you may order directly from the publisher.
Quantity discounts for organizations are available.
Call 1-800-766-8009, toll-free.

ISBN 1-57174-002-3

Printed on acid-free paper in the United States of America

Dedication

To my adolescent sons, Josh and Chad,
who, although difficult at times, were never as
challenging as teens, thankfully, as was I;

and

To Nan, who had to put up with the three of us.

CONTENTS

Response Cost
Consequences, Not Control
Corporal Punishment

Chapter Four

Responsibility ✦ 58

Don't Make the Teen "Even"
Making Responsibility
Learning Responsibility
Responsibility Testing

Chapter Five

Communication ✦ 66

Monopolizing
Lecturing and Preaching
Interrupting
Dismissing or Talking Teens Out of
Their Feelings
Judging
Denying Perceptions
Facilitating Communication—Reflective Listening
Communication as a Tool for Conflict Management
Let Me Get Back To You
Parents United—Even If They Are Wrong
Blended Families
Splitting
Arguing Constructively

Chapter Six

Curfew and Money Matters ✦ 80

Curfew
Money Matters
Allowances
Money and Clothes

Acknowledgement

Thank you to the hundreds of families who trusted me to help them. I learned from them as much as, or more than, I taught them.

INTRODUCTION

Most adults must fulfill three basic responsibilities: do their jobs, be mates, and raise their children. They are usually instructed how to do their work but receive little or no training in how to be successful spouses or effective parents.

To drive a car in this society, one must show that he can at least basically operate a vehicle and pass a written test. To become married, one needs only to find a willing mate and pass a blood test. To become a parent, one must only be biologically capable.

In my first book, *Who's Raising Whom? A Parent's Guide to Effective Child Discipline*, I stressed that parents must learn the *science* of child management. Our greatest resource is our children. We, the older generation, must learn to manage this precious resource wisely. The rising crime rate, epidemic drug abuse, and alarming incidence of divorce and broken families cause one to wonder how well previous generations have raised their children. If we cannot raise our children more effectively than we were raised, we cannot expect the next generation to be more emotionally stable, be happier, or be better parents.

For more than twenty years I have counseled hundreds of parents who are confused, angry, tense, and depressed. They feel they are not in control of their children; that they are not raising their kids but simply reacting to them. As one frustrated parent aptly put it, "I go from putting out one fire to the next—from one crisis to another." It was from working with such parents that I came up with the title *Who's Raising Whom?*

I have never met a child who knows more about raising children than his parents do. This statement is generally true for adolescents as well—but most teenagers would strongly argue this point. Parents must discipline and guide their children and adolescents; they cannot simply react to them.

In my first book, I discussed in detail how parents can *manage* their *children's* behavior. In this book, I refer to parents *coping* with their *adolescents'* behavior. This is an important distinction. Parents can shape, mold, and relatively easily change behavior in their children, especially in younger children. Such is not the case with adolescents. Parents simply do not have the power to significantly alter the behavior of their adolescents. The purpose of this book, then, is to help parents learn to *cope* with and *guide* their adolescents—not necessarily *change* them.

Parents often do not experience major problems with a child until that son or daughter becomes an adolescent. Even if the parents are using marginal management practices, or if the relationship with their child is tenuous, they usually can "keep the lid on" things while the child is young. But when the child reaches adolescence, the normal teenage stresses, coupled with the existing problems, cause the situation to explode.

Parents who "muddle through" with their young children will often "pay the Piper" during their child's adolescence. If they have not learned effective child management skills when their child is young, they likely will have to learn effective coping strategies by the time the child becomes a teenager.

In theory, if parents use the methods I explained in *Who's Raising Whom?* when their children are young, they probably will have fewer problems when their offspring reach adolescence. I often find when working with families that problems the parents are having with their adolescents can be traced to earlier management problems. It does little good, though, to rue the past; we cannot turn back the clock. However, I do frequently recommend to parents of adolescents that they read my first book, even though it was aimed at parents of younger children. *Who's Raising Whom?* reviews important basic management methods and serves as an effective adjunct to methods of dealing with adolescents.

Parents do not have to have an adolescent who is out of control before they read this book. In fact, this book would be very beneficial in helping "normal" families to function even more smoothly.

My wife Nan and I use the techniques discussed in this and my first book in raising our sons, Josh, 17, and Chad, 12. We hope these techniques prove as helpful to you as they have for us.

Larry Waldman

A Typical Scene

Mrs. Sampson comes home from work. As she pulls into the driveway, she notices that the garbage can is still out and the newspapers are not in. She enters the house through an unlocked door. The kitchen is a mess due to her son fixing himself a snack. She can tell what Todd has eaten, as every item—bread, salami, cheese, mustard, mayonnaise, ketchup, pickles—remains on the counter.

She hears loud rock music blaring from Todd's room. She goes there and looks in. Todd is on the phone. She motions for him to turn down the deafening rock crescendo.

Todd's room looks like the aftermath of a tornado. The bathroom is even worse—but Mrs. Sampson hasn't seen that yet. Todd's hair is long and his clothes are strange. She knows that Todd has not begun his homework; his books are still in his book bag even though he has been home for about two hours.

Mrs. Sampson begins yelling at Todd about his irresponsible behaviors. She lists all her concerns: his lack of understanding for the family, his self-centeredness, his poor school performance, his hair, his clothes, his music, his friends, his curfew problem last weekend, and his attitude in general.

Todd, hearing this lecture for the umpteenth time, screams back at his mother and orders her out of the room.

Mrs. Sampson gets in a few more words. As she turns to walk out of the room, she informs Todd that he's "grounded for two weeks!"

Todd slams the door behind his mother and resumes his phone conversation—his friend having listened on the line during this confrontation.

Mrs. Sampson grumbles to herself, and Todd complains to his friend how they are not appreciated or understood.

Chapter One
Adolescence—What Is Normal?

The Peer Group Is Primary

One of the basic—and unfortunate—facts of parenting an adolescent is that parents simply do not have the significant amount of control over the teenager that they did over the child.

During infancy, the child is totally dependent upon its parents for its very survival. During childhood, the youngster models the behavior of the parents. The young child develops much of his or her basic personality traits through this process of imitation. Ask a child of about age ten or less what man or woman that boy or girl admires the most and the answer likely will be "mom" or "dad."

As the child approaches adolescence, this process of idolizing one's parents comes to a screeching halt. Within a matter of months, it often seems, this child, who once was entirely dependent upon his parents for existence, now suddenly changes feelings. The pre-adolescent and adolescent no longer try to imitate their parents or follow their guidelines. Instead, they are totally consumed with modeling their peers. They not only stop following in their parents' footsteps, they often begin to completely reject parental input.

Chad, my 12-year-old, still views me as an all-knowing, all-powerful, infallible father. He becomes visibly upset if I tell him that I am "disappointed" in some aspect of his behavior.

On the other hand, Josh, my teen, sees me as an OK guy who is getting older by the moment, has quite a few "ancient" ideas on how things should be run, has plenty of faults, and tends to dress rather strangely. If I should tell Josh I am unhappy with a particular behavior of his, his attitude is, "So. . .if someone as old, stodgy, and poorly dressed as my father is disappointed in my behavior, that, in fact, might not be such a bad thing."

There were times, when Josh was an early teen, when I happened to compliment him on his outfit—and he turned around and changed his clothes. I'm sure that he thought, "If this old guy thinks I look OK, then probably something is wrong and I had better change."

The adolescent strives to be accepted by his peer group. He tries to dress, look, and behave like his friends. His models become other popular peers and certain rock stars or celebrities who appeal to that age group.

During this process, it is important for parents to understand that they have suffered a significant reduction in their ability to psychologically influence their adolescent offspring. They also have much less physical control as well.

Parents who managed their young children with psychological coercion and/or physical intimidation now find that their ability to direct their teenager using those techniques has been greatly decreased.

I often tell parents that there seems to be a disease associated with raising a teenager. When you have a teenager, for some reason, your intelligence appears to become reduced. Something happens that causes your IQ to decline when your child is in the 13- to 18-year-old range. The good news is that parents surprisingly seem to regain their lost IQ points once their adolescent reaches young adulthood.

Because parents have been afflicted by this "dumb" disease, adolescents often wonder how their parents ever made it this far. The typical adolescents criticize how their parent dress, behave, and think. Not too surprisingly, adolescents often express reservations about being seen in public with such "fools." I noticed within the past year or two that when I would ask Josh if he would like to go with me somewhere, he would always ask for more specific information about our plans. I soon realized that what Josh was really considering was how likely it would be that he would be seen in public with his parents.

When working with parents, I try to impress upon them how the bodies of their adolescent offspring are changing. Teenagers going through puberty are experiencing major hormonal changes and psychological upheavals. Adolescents, while their hormones rage, have sudden growth spurts, suffer with pimples, are subject to tremendous mood swings, and certainly become quite interested in the opposite sex. Not very long ago I told Josh about an article I had read that suggested the average adolescent thought of sex nearly 85 percent of the time. Josh pondered this revelation, then, with a twinkle in his eyes, said, "I wonder what I'm supposed to think about the other 15 percent of the time?"

Along with these major hormonal and physical changes is the timing of going through puberty. The issue with many adolescents is that they need to go through puberty at just the right time. An adolescent who reaches puberty relatively early becomes embarrassed about a suddenly-developing body or new-found hair. On the other hand, an adolescent who is slow in developing and goes through puberty relatively late might be embarrassed about the lack of physical maturity. For many adolescents, it seems that the best thing that could happen is that a group of them could get together, take a vote, and then all go through puberty at the same time and at the same rate.

Josh, as I did, matured early. When he was 11 or 12 he earned the nickname "ape"—presumably because he developed so much body hair before most of his peers. On one hand, Josh seemed proud of his developing body, but at times it also appeared that he was somewhat self-conscious about his early maturation.

Adolescents also have a number of psychological issues to struggle with: for example, choice of friends, how well to function in school, whether to continue their education, choice of careers, and whether to indulge in drugs or other anti-social kinds of acts.

These decisions are very important and stressful at the same time. Adolescents are forced to deal with these concerns while trying to maintain a relationship with their peer reference groups. The typical adolescent is thrust into the situation of having to make these difficult decisions under trying circumstances. It is little wonder that a mountain of stress can envelope teenagers and cause them to become rather impertinent and disturbed at times.

The following anecdote illustrates how stressed and distractible teens can be.

One holiday weekend when Josh was 14, he was asked by our neighbors to watch and feed their dog while they were out of town for several days. On the second day of the job, Josh called me over to the house because the dog had pooped on the carpet. (I theorized to Josh that the dog was angry about being left alone. Josh doubted if any psychology "applied to dogs.") We decided to let the dog out in the back yard for the day and Josh would put the dog back into the house in the evening.

Josh again called me over to the house that evening because the dog was missing. When I pondered aloud how the dog could have escaped, Josh suddenly recalled that the neighbor had mentioned several times before that the dog could jump the fence. I chastised Josh for not remembering that fact before we opted to put the dog in the back yard for the day—a lonely, upset dog at that.

Josh immediately became resigned that the dog ran off and that he would return "when he was ready." I was not so calm. I felt terrible that this beloved dog had disappeared. During the next day and a half I called every animal shelter I could find in an attempt to locate that dog. I even got Josh to put up a few "lost dog" signs in the neighborhood.

On Monday, when the neighbor was to return, I was quite tense because I could not bear telling her that her beloved dog was lost. When she finally called (to thank us) I started to apologize profusely. After 15 seconds, she interrupted me and said, "What are you talking about? Sadie [the dog] is right here." She told me that Sadie had been picked up by her sister on Saturday afternoon, as planned, and that she had explained all of that to Josh several days before she left.

I hung up the phone and marched to Josh's room. I asked him, "Did our neighbor tell you that Sadie would be picked up Saturday afternoon?!"

Josh answered, "Oh, yeah--I forgot."

I could have killed him!! I had worried for a day and a half about a dog that all the time was safe!

Teens certainly can be distractible!!

A major psychological issue with which adolescents deal is that of finding their own identities and seeking their own independence. If you suggest to parents of adolescents that their goal is to raise independent, responsible adults, most parents will quickly agree. The problem is that the parents want their adolescents to become responsible, independent adults—according to the parents' desires. Meanwhile, the adolescents are seeking their own independence and identities and are not necessarily interested in fulfilling their parents' wishes.

The end result of this situation is that adolescents will test limits—of their parents, school, and society—in their efforts to shape their own identities. Obviously, parents must try to curtail some of this limit-testing; however, at the same time, they must be careful not to completely squash it. I often ask parents how many things they did as adolescents that their parents never knew about and are probably glad they never learned about. Most parents usually smile and agree that some testing of limits by adolescents is normal and is, therefore, to be expected.

It might well be that the reason the rooms of most adolescents look like bombs recently went off in them is due, not to inherent slobbiness of the adolescents, but to, at least in part, the adolescents' desire to carve out their own domains.

In *Who's Raising Whom?* I pointedly stated that children misbehave because they are seeking parental attention. Adolescents, on the other hand, misbehave primarily not because they are seeking parental attention, but mainly because they are following their peers, seeking their own independence, are naturally moody or, possibly, are "getting even" with their parents.

Common Traps For Parents

After working for many years with families, I have come to recognize three basic traps into which parents of adolescents often fall:

1. "Last Shot"

When some parents sense that their child is becoming an adult, they don't particularly like what they see in their adolescent. They decide that, in the few remaining years the child is living at home, they will do their best to "shape him up." What the parents are really saying is, "This is my *last shot* before he leaves home."

Certainly the parents' perspective is understood. No one will fault them for trying to "improve" their child before he leaves home. Unfortunately, the situation does not allow for this "last shot."

As we have discussed, the typical adolescent is in the midst of seeking his own identity and searching for his independence and is not particularly influenced by his parents. Parents must understand that, despite their noble goal, attempting to increase their control and management of their adolescent shortly before he leaves home will be met with fierce resistance.

The timing is very wrong. Trying to over-correct adolescents at the exact time they are least receptive to parental input is an exercise in futility.

2. "Letting Go"

This trap ensnares many parents when they realize their child is about to become an adult. This probably occurs more with female adolescents than with males.

Parents who have difficulty in letting go of their child as she approaches adulthood begin to over-correct, add restrictions, and generally try to delay the adolescent's development. Here again, the adolescent vigorously opposes the parents' restrictiveness.

3) "Disciplining the *Child*"

Probably the most common and problematic trap I find in families occurs when parents have not adjusted their parenting styles to coincide with their maturing adolescent.

It is possible, although perhaps not advisable, to coerce a young child or demand that a young child behave or be responsible. Many parents continue to use similar techniques of demands, intimidation, or coercion to raise their teenagers. Trying to raise teenagers using the same methods as when they were little children simply will not work.

A young child might respond, although reluctantly, to a parent who uses coercion or intimidation as a parenting tool. The adolescent, on the other hand, will not tolerate those tenuous parenting techniques. If the typical adolescent feels intimidated, he often will retaliate in a confrontative way or, at a minimum, respond in a more subtle—but passive—aggressive fashion.

The sad but true fact that parents must come to appreciate—if they are not to fall into one of these common traps—is that you cannot make an adolescent do anything he or she does not want to do! When I tell parents this I often get resistance, as many parents are committed to "*making* their teenager become responsible."

I firmly believe that if parents engage in direct forcing of responsible behavior in their adolescent, the end result will be a battle of wills that will satisfy no one.

Parents sometimes accuse me of recommending that they abdicate their roles as leaders or models. This certainly is not the case! I do not at all recommend to parents that they abdicate their roles as parents. I strongly believe that parents can play a strong role in the lives of their adolescents, but they, as parents, must develop management techniques other than coercion, intimidation, or over-correction.

Some time ago a single mother came to me for counseling. She expressed deep concern over her 17-year-old son, who was behaving in a rather irresponsible manner. One, among many, of Tim's irresponsible behaviors was his failure to attend school on a prompt and regular basis. After hearing mom tell me how for years she had cajoled Tim to get to school on time—with poor success—I finally had to tell mom that her efforts were probably of little value in this regard.

Mom, of course, was not at all pleased by my remarks and chose, instead, to increase her efforts at control. For the next two to three weeks she awakened Tim early, cajoled him out of bed, nagged him to wash up, urged him to get dressed, forced him to eat breakfast, demanded that he get into the car, drove him to school, walked him to his first-hour class, and then stood outside the classroom door for the first 15 minutes or so. The result of all of Mom's work was that Tim waited for her to leave and them simply exited the classroom and school for the day. Mom demanded that the school keep Tim in class, but a school official responded by saying that their institution was not a prison.

Several weeks later, mom came back to me and reluctantly abided by my philosophy. She was finally ready to discuss ways of dealing with Tim other than through coercion.

Unrealistic Standards

Often I ask parents, especially the father, "What were you like as an adolescent?"

A common response is, "Oh, I was really something! If my kid acted like I did when I was his age, I'd kill him!"

Is that fair? I don't believe so. I'm not saying that our kids should be at least as bad as we were as children, but is it appropriate to hold our kids to unrealistic standards? Most adults enjoy talking about their escapades in their youth—and most adults turn out OK. The fact is that most of today's adolescents, as crazy as they might seem, will eventually grow up to be responsible, tax-paying, even conservative adults.

Our expectations of standards concerning our teens, therefore, must be realistic.

Separate—and Healthy

At times I see parents who act as if *they* were the ones who received the bad grade or got the detention. These parents feel personally insulted when their child gets into any kind of trouble. These parents believe that their child's behavior is a direct reflection of their self-worth and ability as parents. Many times I have to ask, "Whose report card is this?"

These parents are considered by mental health professionals to be *enmeshed* with their children and often try to live their children's lives for them. It might be satisfying to completely direct a child's life, but I don't know many teens who would allow it. Our children are not our clones. We should shape and guide them, but ultimately we must let them experience life for themselves. Therefore, sometimes being more separate is healthy. Psychologists call this *individuation.*

The summer before my freshman year of high school, my family moved from the west (working-class) side of Milwaukee to the east (Yuppie) side. For me it was quite a cultural shift. Most of my social life for the first two to three years of high school was with "my west-side friends." I did, however, marry Nan—an east-side girl.

I remember looking fondly at several east-side girls in their expensive coordinated outfits. I felt, then, that somehow I was beneath them and that there was no way they would be interested in dating a west-side boy like me.

I used to share some of my feelings with my parents, and they always used to say the same thing: "You're a nice boy. You're intelligent and good looking. [I guess they were right there!] Ask one of them out. What do you have to lose?"

I remember always answering them, "You just don't understand! I'm from the west side; these girls don't like guys from the wrong side of the tracks."

Twenty years later, I was at my 20th high school reunion. (I won't say how long ago that was!) I happened to be sitting with two of the "hottest" (then) girls in my class. (They both still looked pretty good.) With considerably more self-esteem than I possessed two decades before, I proceeded to tell these two attractive women that 20 years or so ago I would have given up an important part of my anatomy to be with these two ladies. But, because of the west-side issue, I never approached them.

Simultaneously, both said, "Larry, I always thought you were nice. I would have been delighted to go out with you."

That moment hit me hard—personally and professionally. On a personal level, I realized at that instant that my parents were right—again. Professionally, I once more recognized that you cannot change a teen's view *with the facts*; if a teen believes something, even if it's wrong, you are not likely to change it.

It took me over 20 years.

Important Points To Remember in Chapter One

1. Parents must accept that they have significantly less influence over their teen than when he was a child.

2. The adolescent's peer group has more influence than do the parents.

3. Considerable emotional and physical changes occur in the adolescent.

4. Seeking their identities, teens naturally challenge parents and authority figures.

5. Parents should avoid the traps of "Last Shot," "Letting Go" or "Disciplining the *Child.*"

6. Parents' expectations regarding their teens must be realistic.

7. You cannot make teens do things they do not choose to do.

"Sometimes when I look at my children I say to myself, 'Lillian, you should have stayed a virgin.'"

Mrs. Lillian Carter

Chapter Two
Basic Coping Techniques

Positive Reinforcement

Positive reinforcement is the use of something reward-
ing or desirable following a particular appropriate behavior that should increase the odds of that behavior
continuing.

Reinforcement needs to be relatively immediate. It also
must be specific. Reinforcement is most effective when
used immediately after a desired behavior. By specifying
the specific behavior that is being reinforced, the parent
teaches the child what particular behavior gets rewarded.

Reinforcement is effective because it provides an *incentive* and *educates* the child about what he can *do* to earn
a reward.

In *Who's Raising Whom?* I stressed that positive reinforcement serves as the cornerstone for child management, mainly because the young child craves the parent's
attention. If the parent teaches the child that essentially
only good behavior will get recognition, then in time the
child will behave appropriately.

Adolescents, however, are not nearly as desirous of
their parents' attention. In fact, many teenagers would
prefer to have their parents leave them alone altogether.
Even so, the use of positive reinforcement remains very
important in coping with the adolescent.

As noted in the previous chapter, it is quite difficult to
make an adolescent do something he does not choose to

do. Behaving in an appropriate, responsible manner is a choice that must be made by the adolescent. The use of positive reinforcement by the parent, however, can *encourage* the adolescent to often make that appropriate choice.

All too often I meet with parents who complain bitterly that their adolescent is functioning in a disrespectful, irresponsible manner. When I ask them what kinds of things they do with their adolescent for fun, the response I often get is, "We hardly, if ever, do anything together for fun. Who would want to?"

At that point, I try to get the parents to understand that if the adolescent perceives them as simply taskmasters or slave drivers, then it is unlikely that the adolescent will quickly and easily comply with their wishes. The nature of the relationship between adolescent and parents determines, to a large degree, the level of responsible behavior exhibited by the adolescent.

Give To Get

A highly successful executive reluctantly came to see me because his 12-year-old son Kevin was failing to complete his homework despite being a capable student. The executive informed me how very busy he was, how he really did not have time for me, and how, frankly, he did not put much stock in psychology.

(I thought we were just getting off to a wonderful start!)

The father related how he had responded to Kevin's irresponsible behavior by a series of punishments and losses of privileges. After speaking for about 45 minutes, he abruptly said, "What should I do about this?"

I said, "Take Kevin bowling."

He glared incredulously. "I knew you types were of no help! What does bowling have to do with Kevin's problem?!"

I told him that if how he related to me in that session was any indication of the nature of his relationship with his son, I could understand Kevin's behavior. I suggested that Kevin was angry because his father did not spend any time with him other than to announce punishments. (To tell you the truth, I was getting rather perturbed with the father myself.) I argued that Kevin was most likely retaliating against him by means of irresponsible behaviors that he knew would drive his old man up the wall. Negative attention is better than no attention at all.

The father, during his non-stop "relating," had mentioned how much Kevin had enjoyed going bowling with him once or twice in the past. Therefore, I recommended that:

(1) he needed to continue to see me on a regular basis; and

(2) he take Kevin bowling to show Kevin that his father was not simply a slave driver but rather someone with whom his son could have fun.

Four weeks and several bowling sessions later, this father reported that his relationship with his son had begun to improve and that Kevin was becoming more responsible about his homework.

The lesson this father learned was "Give to get."

If our adolescents are to behave responsibly and meet our demands, we parents must extend ourselves and our *time* to them.

Most parents realize that it is important to spend quality time with young children; however, many parents tend to give relatively little quality time to their teens. As problems arise, the parents tend to spend even less time with their teens. To get adolescents to become responsible, the parents must *give some quality time* to them.

No News Is Good News

During two decades of counseling with families, I've

come to believe that many families seem to live under an unspoken premise. It seems that an imaginary sign has been posted above the front doors of many homes. That sign says, "No news is good news."

Many families apparently operate under the assumption that if you hear no complaining, then things are going well. An example is a young couple who came to me for marital counseling. In their early twenties, they had been married only two and a half years. I asked the husband, "How can you tell when things are going well with you and your wife?"

I thought this was a difficult question that would lead to some therapeutic discussion. Instead, the husband shot back, "That's simple. I can tell we're getting along when she isn't bitching at me!"

(What a wonderful way to live, I thought, to know that you and your wife are getting along when you're not being criticized or yelled at!)

This marriage, it seemed, operated under the unspoken premise, "Assume I love you—unless you hear different!"

Most families operate in this fashion. What gets talked about at the dinner table? Is it how well mom prepared or cooked dinner? How nicely she has cleaned the car? How well dad has kept the yard? How nicely the kids have done their homework? Or how well things, in general, are going?

Rarely.

Instead, what usually gets the recognition and the attention are the things that seem to be going badly. It is most unfortunate that in many homes little attention is paid to things that are going well.

Operating under the sign "No news is good news" with your adolescents is a sure way to get into trouble with them.

Extinction

In behavioral treatment, *extinction* is the counterpart to reinforcement. With reinforcement the parent selectively attends to particular appropriate behaviors in the child.

With extinction, the parent selectively ignores particular inappropriate behaviors. The theory behind extinction is that when the parent does not pay attention to inappropriate behavior, the child's misbehavior will stop, become "extinguished," due to the lack of attention and reinforcement.

Extinction techniques are especially useful with younger children because, as we have discussed, the child craves the parent's attention. Using a systematic combination of reinforcement and extinction, the child will soon decrease the ignored inappropriate behavior and increase the approved appropriate behavior.

Since adolescents are not as desirous of their parents' attention, extinction is perhaps not quite as effective as a behavioral change tool, but it is certainly still useful.

Making Your Goat Less Gettable

While adolescents might not be quite so interested in their parents' approval, they many times seek their parents' attention for no reason other than to "get their parents' goat."

Teenagers naturally become unhappy or upset when they are told they are not allowed to do something, are asked to complete a chore, or are disciplined. Since they are nearly as verbal as their parents—in some cases even more so—they try to argue their points or negotiate to their advantage. The end result is that parents become embroiled in arguments, shouting often ensues, and everyone becomes angry and frustrated.

The majority of these confrontations conclude with the parent declaring, "I am your mother/father and you will do it because I told you so!!!" To which the adolescent yells out something unpleasant, stomps out, and slams the bedroom door. The parent, extremely frustrated, goes to the medicine cabinet looking for something to ease an upset stomach and splitting headache.

Over the years of counseling with adolescents, I often

asked them, "How often do you manage to argue your point successfully with your parents?" The vast majority of teens have reported to me that seldom do they win arguments with their folks. After they respond to my question I then ask, "If you are usually unsuccessful arguing with your parents, why do you persist in doing so?" Most teens do not have a good reply.

The answer, I believe, is simple. While the teen might recognize that he might not persuade the parents, at least by arguing with them he gains the satisfaction of seeing the parents become angry and frustrated. In essence, the adolescent's motto is, "You anger me, so I upset you."

By appropriately using extinction, parents prevent their "goat from getting gotten." I continually tell parents of adolescents to not try to persuade their offspring or expect them to say that they agree with the parents, are sorry for what they did, or will do exactly what the parent requested. It just won't happen!! Inform the adolescent briefly and concisely of your point and then walk away.

Often when teens are disciplined or told to do something they yell back, "I won't do it!" Most of the time they are simply frustrated, are letting off steam—and are inviting the parent into a shouting match.

Use extinction in these cases: ignore the outburst and in most instances the adolescent will, grudgingly, do what was requested.

Controlling Your Temper When Your Teen Is Losing It

Adolescents are notoriously moody. A common mistake parents of teens make is that they allow their teen's mood to dictate theirs. This is hard on the adult's emotional system.

When Josh was an early teen, as his hormones began flowing (and they never stopped), he was quite labile. He would turn from being cheerful to irritable back to being calm all within minutes.

I recall one early evening when Nan and I had a nice brief chat in our bedroom. She then left the room and went into the kitchen where she apparently met Josh. Within about 45 seconds I began to hear terrible screaming and shouting. As I rushed toward the kitchen, Josh walked brusquely past me on his way to his room muttering something under his breath about his "mean mom."

In the kitchen Nan was standing there looking like she was about to break something. Her blood pressure was probably about double its normal level. We talked a bit about what had just transpired. I then noted to her that in less than a minute she had gone from being relaxed and calm to nearly having a stroke. We then agreed that we were not going to let Josh's adolescent moodiness make us crazy.

Who is in control of your emotions? Only yourself, of course.

Parents must work at controlling their feelings and not allow a labile teen to direct the mood of the house. If a teen chooses to be upset, that will have to be his problem. Nowhere is it written that a parent's mood must match that of the teen.

Adults typically do not change emotions as fast as do teens. We parents tend to get upset and then stay angry long after the teen has calmed down. Many times the teen cannot understand why we are still so angry—the teen has already forgotten.

Persuasion and Resolution—Lost Fantasies

Parents of adolescents often have problems with arguing. More parents than I can count have complained to me how they spend long, exhausting hours arguing with their teens. I submit that parents have this problem mainly because of a simple misconception: they believe their kids are persuadable.

When two (probably unmarried) adults argue, the implicit assumption is that if a logical, convincing position is expressed, the opposing party will consider that perspective and probably come to accept it. Such is not the case when a parent argues with a child, especially a teen.

The teen is not interested in his parents' point of view and generally is closed to it. The teen argues to win his point, or, at a minimum, to aggravate his parents. If the teen is not persuadable, then why even bother trying?

In all of my years of treating children and their families and raising two children of my own, I've yet to learn of an instance where a parent and a child were arguing and the parent put forth a reasonable, coherent, cogent point of view and the child said, "Thanks for bringing that up—you've convinced me."

Say what needs to be said and close the discussion; do not allow yourself to become embroiled in an unwinnable argument.

Many parents will pursue arguments far past the point of diminishing returns in the hope of some resolution. Often when a married couple argue they ultimately manage to come to some resolution; for example, "I promise to never call your mother that name again." I want to stress again, however, that the reality of finding some resolution with teens rarely exists. The closest I've ever gotten with my adolescent is hearing him say, "I know what you want me to say but I won't say it."

Coming to an agreed-upon resolution to an argument with your adolescent is nice—but very rare. State your message and don't necessarily look for confirmation.

Choosing Your Battleground

A savvy general selects his battlefield carefully. Most parents of adolescents, unfortunately, do not follow this simple advice. Most parents fight their teen "to the death" on every front: hair, clothes, jewelry, chores, food, TV, room, babysitting, school, friends, curfew, money, sex, privileges, *ad nauseam.*

The problem with this situation is that the adolescent cannot differentiate between major and minor issues. While an adolescent male yearning to put a gold stud in his ear lobe can certainly be disconcerting to some parents, it probably does not equate with the teen buying a motorcycle or quitting school.

I recommend to parents that they take an honest inventory of themselves and decide what issues they can live with and what issues they believe are non-negotiable—and, hopefully, winnable. By conceding some minor issues but remaining firm on a few important ones, they will show the adolescent, hopefully, that his parents are reasonable and that possibly mutually acceptable agreements can be reached.

If parents carefully "choose their battlegrounds" and ignore some minor problems, they stand a better chance in getting cooperation from their teen.

Walls

Every time parents issue an edict or a demand, they essentially are putting up a wall that they must defend and support. I often remind parents that the more walls they erect, the more walls they give their adolescent to *push* against. Parents can defend and support only so many walls before they collapse like a house of cards—or the parents become completely frazzled.

Establish only those walls that are necessary but "go to the mat" defending them. In time, your teen will know which walls are impregnable.

Logical Consequences

Logical or natural consequences is a psychological term that refers to the natural or logical balance in our worlds. For example, I *still* cut my grass every weekend (during the Arizona growing season) because if I skip a week, it takes me three times as long to mow it the following week.

Most adults get up and leave on time for work in the morning, even though they might prefer additional beauty rest; they do not get up because their mothers called them and told them to do so. They awaken and get to work responsibly because they know that if they come to work late, they will have to pay some price.

The price we pay for our inappropriate, irresponsible behavior is the *natural* or *logical* consequence. Logical consequences keep most adults on the "righteous road."

Logical consequences would work well for children and adolescents if we allowed them to—but too often we don't.

The use of logical consequences is considered an extension of extinction because by *doing nothing* the parent allows the teen to see the consequences of his or her irresponsible behavior. The appropriate use of logical consequences is, next to reinforcement, one of the most powerful ways a parent can influence and cope with the adolescent's behavior.

In my earlier book, I referred to logical consequences in situations where a young child might become embarrassed by going to school undressed if he procrastinates in the morning, or be upset if he misses his dinner because he fails to come home on time. With adolescents we are likely dealing with weightier issues than procrastination, coming home late for dinner, or "picking at your peas." Instead, parents of teens are concerned with issues such as curfew, school work, irresponsibility, and drugs.

As I already suggested, it is fruitless to compel your teen to do something he chooses not to do. The obvious course of action, then, is logical consequences: the logical consequence of coming home late is that the teen misses dinner or must cook his own; the logical consequence of staying up too late is that the teen is tired and uncomfortable the next day; the logical consequence for breaking curfew is that the parents cannot trust the teen to take the car out the next weekend; the consequence for cutting a class is that the school is informed and the teen must face the teacher's wrath and receive an F for that class that day; the consequence for failing to come to work is that the teen is terminated from his job; the failure to complete homework and study results in unsatisfactory grades and possibly the need to repeat that grade the next school year.

In all of these examples, and in many more, the teen behaves inappropriately and the parents, gripping their seat and gritting their teeth, do not rant and rave; they simply *allow* the logical consequences of the inappropriate act to be felt.

I am not saying that the parents simply sit idly by and say nothing. The parents should clearly and *calmly* explain their disappointment in the teen's behavior and clearly give the teen their recommendation.

The essential point, though, is that teens must be allowed to clearly see the end result of their inappropriate or irresponsible behavior. Teens must relate to the *consequences* of their acts and not primarily to their parents' *anger and frustration.*

For years I have said that it is far better for children to see the consequences of their irresponsibility early in their lives rather than to experience such failure as adults.

Josh was extremely excited the day we went to apply for his driver's license—too excited. I knew he needed his birth certificate—which had purposely been set aside on the desk for him—but Josh had not responsibly put it in with the necessary papers. I asked Josh twice if he had reviewed the manual, especially the front page which listed the required paperwork (including the birth certificate).

Josh brushed me off and said he knew everything from his driver's ed training, so he didn't have to go read the pamphlet. He wanted to go and be the first in line that morning. Well, we left without the birth certificate. We were second in line. When the clerk asked the teen who was first in line for his birth certificate to confirm his age, he and Josh simultaneously shrieked, "Oh, no! I forgot!"

Since I was unwilling to take another hour from work due to Josh's irresponsibility, Josh rode his bike "ten miles each way" the next day and obtained his license. (By the way, since he has been able to drive he hasn't ridden his bike that far ever since.)

Both my sons know that, when we're about to leave the house and I say, "Do we have everything?" they had better be sure. They stop, think, and check because they know their father isn't going to go back to save them.

Using logical consequences is an excellent tactic.

Owning the Problem

I often ask parents to closely examine whether the problem at hand is owned by their teen or themselves. Frequently the problem is primarily owned by the teen; for example, grades, hygiene, clothes, and bedtime. When the problem is primarily owned by the adolescent, generally parents are best off trying to allow logical consequences to have their inevitable effect.

When a teen *chooses* to behave inappropriately or irresponsibly and suffers the inevitable logical consequences for his act, it is most important that the parent calmly point out to the teen the errors of his way.

Many times I've asked Josh, "What lesson did we learn from this?" If the parents become excessively angry and upset—while they certainly might be entitled to—the teen will likely respond to the parent's anger rather than to the logical consequence of the teen's behavior.

Therefore, parents must remain relatively calm and help the teen learn to recognize the irresponsibility of his act.

Parents typically assume that if their child or teen misbehaves, the parenting process has been a failure. This might not at all be the case.

In behavior therapy, progress proceeds one of two ways. One way is for the patient (in this case the child or teen) to behave appropriately and get reinforced for good behavior. Everybody is pleased in this situation—the parent gets the desired behavior and the child or teen gets rewarded.

In the second case, the child or teen misbehaves and is either ignored by the parent or allowed to suffer the logical consequence of his inappropriate act. Clearly no one is particularly happy with this situation—the parent is displeased with the poor behavior and the child or teen dislikes being ignored or having to deal with the natural consequence of irresponsibility.

Nevertheless, from a therapeutic perspective, a good thing happened. It is just as therapeutic for a teen to misbehave and be ignored or suffer a logical consequence as it is for a teen to behave appropriately and be reinforced—perhaps even more so.

Parents should not be discouraged by occasional lapses in their teen's behavior. Parents, instead, should view these situations as opportunities for alternative therapeutic learning to occur.

Some time ago I was working with a mother regarding her two children. After the second session, it became clear that the major problem in that home was not the children but Dad—who was drinking alcohol to excess. Father was unwilling to address his problems and preferred to blame his wife and children for his drinking.

Mother and I developed an intervention plan similar in concept to the one we used with her children. If Father returned home from work by six o'clock and had not stopped to drink, Mother tried to cook him a nice dinner and be more sensitive to his needs. If Father came home late or drunk, Mother simply packed up the children and went to Grandmother's house for the night. She no longer argued or fought with him and was now unable to call work the next morning and say he had "the flu."

In a few weeks, Father's drinking was significantly reduced. Mother learned that it was necessary and effective to allow Father to experience, firsthand, what happens when he drinks. She stopped viewing his drinking as her failure but as another therapeutic opportunity. Dad ultimately sought help.

Important Points To Remember in Chapter Two

1. The responsibility level of teens is largely determined by the nature of the relationships between them and their parents.

2. Parents must spend some quality time with their teens—give to get.

3. Do not let the labile adolescent's mood determine yours—control your "goat."

4. Adolescents are not persuadable. Do not expect resolution in arguments.

5. Concede minor issues but remain firm on major ones—choose your battlegrounds.

6. Teens must relate to the consequences of their acts and not primarily to their parents' anger and frustration.

"There are only two things a child will share willingly—communicable diseases and his mother's age."

Dr. Benjamin Spock

Chapter Three
Punishment

As I argued in *Who's Raising Whom?* punishment is not a particularly effective method to alter children's behavior. Often the primary effect of punishment is to make the punishee (the child) more watchful of the punisher (the parent).

For example, research has clearly shown that the long-term effect of receiving a ticket for speeding is not an overall reduction in speed; rather, the driver becomes more conscious of where the police are stationed.

Similarly, adolescents tend to become resentful—*and revengeful*—when punishment is applied. Therefore, punishment needs to be used sparingly with teens and when it is used it must be administered appropriately.

As we've seen, positive reinforcement, extinction, and using logical consequences are generally more effective than punishment in influencing children's and adolescents' behavior, and these techniques should be tried first.

I often tell parents that when they see inappropriate behavior in their kids, they should ask themselves these questions: (1) What would I prefer them to do instead? and (2) Is it worth fighting for? If the parent can specifically answer the first question, then the parent can reinforce the alternative desired behavior.

A while back I was driving on the freeway and I happened to glance at the car next to me. In that car was a family: father and mother in the front seat and two boys, about seven and nine, in the back seat. As Dad was driving on the crowded highway, he was swinging his right arm behind him trying to hit his two sons. I noted the boys were giggling and intermittently ducking behind the seat to avoid Father's blows. (I smiled and thought it was always nice to see prospective clients.)

Apparently this father wanted his kids to sit quietly in the back seat and apparently he chose to try to use corporal punishment to elicit that behavior. Obviously he was not getting good results.

Besides punishment—corporal punishment, no less— what else might that father have done to get the behavior he was looking for?

1. He could have reinforced the behavior he was looking for: "If you guys can sit still and quiet, when we get off the freeway we will stop and all have a soda."

2. He could have distracted the kids and reinforced a more appropriate behavior: "Let's play a game. The first one to spot ten out-of-state licenses is a winner!" Reinforcing alternative desired behavior can be effective.

Obviously if the parent decides the misbehavior isn't worth fighting for, then the best response is probably no response at all. In my experience, if parents take the time to consider whether the misbehavior is worth a response, they usually recognize it isn't.

Most minor misbehaviors are best dealt with by ignoring them. Nevertheless, there certainly will be times when punishment with a teen should be considered.

Goals of Punishment

For punishment to be effective at all, parents must keep in focus the basic objective of the technique. By failing to consider the aims of punishment, parents often do a poor job of discipline.

The primary goals of punishment are to *alert* the child that some behavior is unacceptable, to *stop* that misbehavior, and to attempt to *ensure* that the misbehavior does not reoccur. These objectives can be accomplished only if the parent generally remains *calm* while administering the punishment.

If the parent becomes excessively angry or excitable, as we too often do, the child or adolescent responds to the parent's emotion and not to the resulting penalty. The punishment, therefore, becomes ineffective—the message gets lost in the medium. Screaming at an adolescent will likely return ranting and raving; little positive benefit will result from such interaction.

Kim, 15, was caught in his private school smoking marijuana. The school handled the situation by not allowing him to return the following semester. He had to finish the year at a public school and if he "kept his nose clean" he could return to the school the next fall.

Kim's father was understandably angry. He was so angry that for weeks after the incident he rarely spoke to his son and if he did say something it was negative.

I saw this family three weeks after the incident. Kim, it seemed to me, was more angry at his father's reaction than he was concerned about his own misdeed. (Some of this was probably an emotional defense to deny or diffuse some of his guilt.) I noted to Father that he was "confusing the signals" with his excessive anger. While I reflected that he had every right to be angry, I suggested that he tone down his anger and allow Kim to directly and clearly feel his guilt and see the consequences of his irresponsible act.

Kim finished the year at an alternative school and returned to his private school and did well and stayed clean. He and his father, I believe, became closer over the incident. Kim learned two important lessons: his father could forgive him; and "don't do the crime unless you are ready to do the time."

I often point out to parents that punishment is not revenge or retribution. It is not a basic tenet of punishment theory to make the teen at least as upset as is the parent. Besides, most teens will not give the parents the satisfaction of letting them know that the punishment "got to them." Don't expect it.

Several years ago, a mother with whom I was working called me and complained that an intervention that we had designed for her 13-year-old son was "not working." When I asked her how she knew the program was not effective, she reported, "Whenever I apply the punishment, Brad says, 'I don't care!'"

I then asked her how often she was seeing Brad's inappropriate behavior that we were trying to reduce. She responded by saying that the misbehavior was "probably less than before."

What was this woman considering? Was she interested in having the misbehavior decrease or having her son complain more about the punishment she was administering? Remember, parents should attend to their teen's *behavior,* not his attitude.

Rules of Punishment

There are several rules of punishment that parents of adolescents should follow:

1. Be calm and matter-of-fact to allow the goals of punishment to remain in focus.

2. Punish immediately. The closer the connection between the punishment and the misbehavior, the more effective the punishment. One of the basic civil rights is the right to a speedy trial. Such is also the case with punishment. Telling a teen "Wait till dad/mom gets home," is not appropriate. Besides, it sends the message that the parent in charge is incapable of handling the problem. Moreover, it tends to ruin Dad's/Mom's homecoming as well. The rule of immediacy also applies to the length of punishment—but more on that later.

3. Be specific. The teen must understand clearly and specifically what he did that was wrong. Remember, it is difficult to correct "a bad attitude"—whatever that is.

4. Be able to enforce the punishment. I have seen many parents apply punishments that they could not realistically enforce. Telling a teen that he cannot associate with a particular peer is probably a lost cause. Most teens leave for school early in the morning and do not return home until late afternoon. On weekends they might be gone from home even longer. How can the parent ensure that the teen is not, in fact, interacting with a non-preferred peer?

Insisting that your teen comply with an unenforceable demand only sets up the teen to lie to you. Surely the parent should explain (briefly) why it is preferred that the teen not keep company with a non-desirable peer, but to insist on it when there is no way to enforce it is useless—and might even be harmful.

Recently I began working with a single mother of a 12-year-old, Tim. When Tim misbehaved, mother disciplined him by withdrawing his TV privileges for a week. Unfortunately, since mother worked long hours, she had little ability to monitor Tim's TV watching. Often when she came home from work at 6:00 or 6:30 P.M. the TV was off, but warm, even hot! Obviously, Mother's punishment was unenforceable. Tim was being induced to be deceitful with her.

5. Keep the punishment brief. With respect to young children, I stress that punishments should last no longer than the remainder of that day. With teens, most punishments should probably last no more than through the following weekend or for, at most, a week. However, for something flagrant, like taking the car without permission, for example, loss of driving privileges for a month or two might be in order. For most common infractions, such as talking back, breaking curfew, failing to complete an important assignment or chore, or ditching a class, a punishment spanning several days, up to a week, is usually appropriate.

Remember, the objective of punishment is not retribution or revenge. Punishment does not have to be greatly upsetting to the teen to be effective.

If a teen is punished for too long a time for an infraction or is made to become too upset, the teen stops thinking about his or her misdeed and simply becomes angry. The teen is now more likely to think about getting even than about the irresponsible behavior.

I have seen adolescents whose parents have restricted them from TV, the phone, the stereo, etc., for an entire report card period (nine weeks). This extended type of punishment rarely results in a teen changing behavior. Instead, the teen often simply gives up, feels there is nothing to work for, or becomes extremely angry and the situation worsens. When I work with teens in this predicament, there is little left to use as incentive to encourage new responsible behavior.

Types of Punishment

Different types of punishment are appropriate for children of different ages. Overcorrection (requiring the repetition of a repeatable inappropriate behavior) and time-out (sending the child to his room) can be quite effective for youngsters, but these techniques would be rather demeaning and inappropriate for adolescents.

I-Message

In assertiveness training, individuals are taught to clearly express their feelings without resorting to accusations, criticism, and yelling. This concept is often referred to as an *I-message*.

As noted in my first book, younger children often will respond well to I-messages because they greatly value the parents' attention and want to stay in the parents' good graces. Although the adolescent does not care nearly as much about the parent's attention, an assertive, calm, non-inflammatory I-statement often will change the teen's behavior.

Recently, I learned that Josh had made what was considered to be a smart-aleck comment to one of his teachers. When I learned of the incident, I sat down with Josh and told him, calmly and briefly, in a non-threatening manner, that I was embarrassed by and disappointed in his behavior.

Josh, of course, was not happy with my words and began to try to give an alibi and defend himself. I simply restated what I heard and how I felt and walked away. The following day, Josh related to me that he had apologized to his Spanish teacher. I let him know that I thought that was a good move.

Telling a teen what one *sees* or *hears* and how one *feels* can lead to a behavior change. Unlike a child, the teen needs to save face and probably will wait a bit—possibly a day or two—before changing the behavior.

At the very least, with an I-message the parent clearly communicates to the teen how he feels about a particular misbehavior.

Response Cost

Penalizing a teen for a particular inappropriate behavior is technically defined as *response cost*. When administering response cost, the parent must keep in mind all the aforementioned guidelines: react in a non-inflammatory manner, be specific about the misdeed, make the penalty brief, and be sure the punishment is enforceable.

As our children age, the enforceability of punishments becomes more difficult. Most teens leave home early in the morning for school and return home late in the day, and many parents are also rather busy; thus, it is difficult to continually enforce many penalties consistently for extended periods of time (which is another reason why they should be short).

Parents should not put themselves into positions where they are wrestling the phone out of the teen's hand or barring the door to prevent the teen from leaving the house. If the teen grudgingly accepts a restriction from the phone or a grounding, fine; but if the teen blatantly continues to use the phone or defiantly leaves the house after being grounded, obviously some other enforceable penalties must be enacted.

Some penalties parents typically always can enforce are: withholding allowance, removal of the phone in the teen's room, confiscating the Nintendo module, locking the doors if the teen leaves inappropriately or is past curfew, disinviting the teen from a family outing or a trip, refusing to pay car insurance, termination of car insurance, calling the police if the teen takes the car without permission.

With children, punishment is used primarily to discontinue inappropriate behavior. With adolescents, punishment is unlikely to significantly alter behavior but it generally sends a clear signal that a particular misbehavior is not acceptable.

Parents often become frustrated when a particular punishment "doesn't work." I frequently remind parents that no punishment, short of doing great bodily harm, will definitely cause a certain misbehavior to cease. There are no guarantees in this arena. Punishment simply clearly dictates to the teen that a particular misdeed is unacceptable and that if the teen exhibits that inappropriate behavior again, the teen will likely receive an enforceable consequence.

Hopefully, with the consistent use of reinforcement and extinction techniques and the propitious use of punishment methods, parents will be able to influence and cope with their teen's behavior.

Consequences. Not Control.

Parents of adolescents often come to me in the hope that somehow I will be able to make their teen do something the teen doesn't choose to do. I wonder at times what magical power parents think I possess that enables me to cause teens to change when the parents, with all the authority and time, haven't been able to make the teen's behavior change.

Coercing teens to change when they don't care to is a fruitless task. I believe parents exhaust and frustrate themselves when they try to force their teen to change and/or when they want to control nearly every aspect of their teen's behavior. Obviously, parents are not in position to control most of their teen's behavior. As noted, adolescents do not tolerate parental over-control very well; also, they are simply out of the house a great deal and not available to be controlled.

While parents cannot *control* most of their teen's behavior, parents certainly have the authority and the opportunity to apply *consequences* for behavior. In essence, it is not so important what the teen does; it is far more important what *consequences* the parent applies to the behavior the teen has chosen to exhibit.

I see many parents that are "stuck" because they are set on *making* their teen do the right thing. Of course, wanting your child to behave appropriately is admirable, but insisting that your teen do something is wasteful.

Typically I counsel parents that they should convey their feelings to their teen but then allow their teen to decide how he will behave. Once the teen acts, the parent can follow through with a consequence: reinforce a responsible choice; ignore a mildly inappropriate behavior and allow a logical consequence to occur; and punish, if necessary, a more serious negative choice.

Again, it is not so important what the adolescent does; rather, it is much more important what the parent does after the teen has acted.

Corporal Punishment

In *Who's Raising Whom?* I strongly argue against corporal punishment. Any type of punishment is the least-preferred tool, to be used largely as a last resort—and corporal punishment is especially not preferred and not effective. Spanking sets up the situation where the parent is providing intense attention to the child at the worst time—when the child (or teen) has seriously misbehaved.

If parents overuse physical punishment, they tend to become committed to it, which creates frustration and anger on both sides. Kids in this situation then behave only under the threat of discipline.

Corporal punishment with teens is absolutely ineffective. Hitting teens squashes their self-esteem, makes them terribly angry, and, most importantly, loses the focus on the misdeed. Remember, your teen might be as strong or soon might be stronger than you. One certainly does not want to have physical confrontations under such circumstances.

Corporal punishment has no place in coping with adolescents; not only is it ineffective—it's foolish.

Important Points To Remember in Chapter Three

1. Before using punishment, parents should consider what behavior they would prefer instead—and whether the misbehavior is worth fight over.

2. For punishment to be effective, it must be administered calmly, immediately, specifically, and briefly, and it should be enforceable.

3. Although punishment might not change behavior, it sends the clear message that certain

misbehaviors are unacceptable and will have consequences.

4. It is not so important what the teen does; it is
   much more important what the parent does after
   the teen has acted.

5. Corporal punishment has no place in coping with
   the adolescent.

"The young always have the same problem—how to rebel and conform at the same time. They now have solved this by defying their parents and copying one another."

Quentin Crisp

Chapter Four

Responsibility

More often than not, one of the major problems—if not *the major problem*—parents have with their teens concerns the issue of *responsibility*. Most parents complain that their teens are not responsible for their household chores, school homework, and many other obligations. Often parents react to the situation by nagging their teens to be responsible, harshly criticizing their irresponsible behavior, and punishing them.

Such tactics rarely are effective. Any teen who is being nagged, criticized, or punished for irresponsible behavior is very unlikely to strive to become more responsible. In most cases, the teen will become angry. Angry teens either will withdraw (isolate), act out (be angry) or behave in a passive-aggressive manner (retaliating in an indirect, manipulative fashion). Most irresponsible teens express their displeasure with their parents by continuing to be irresponsible. They rarely become responsible when coerced.

I recall a session I had with a frustrated mother of a 15-year-old daughter. Mother lamented, "I have to wake Sarah up in the morning; I have to make her get dressed; I have to make her eat breakfast; I have to remind her to get her books; I have to get her out to the bus on time; when is this girl going to learn some responsibility?!!"

Guess what? Sarah will begin developing responsibility when she is given the opportunity to do so.

Don't Make the Teen "Even"

When parents ask their teen to do a task or chore, the adolescent is somewhat obligated; he owes something (in the form of a deed) to the parent.

As we all know so very well, many teens will procrastinate or perhaps argue when given a chore. What is a parent most likely to do? He proceeds to yell, scream, threaten, demean, or coerce. The teen now, of course, feels angry. In fact, any "debt" he felt he might have owed to the parent is certainly canceled. While he might have felt slightly obligated when first asked to do something by his parents, after being screamed at and criticized harshly, he then feels he has more than paid the debt; he now has little or no remorse at all for not fulfilling his parent's task.

The parent, in this situation, has "made the adolescent *even.*"

Ask the teen calmly to do a specific task. Do not argue and do not stand there and insist that the job get done instantly—unless it is absolutely mandatory that it be done immediately. Let the weight of the request or obligation rest on the teen. While this tactic certainly does not guarantee that the teen will be responsible, it at least assures that the parents do not provide the teen with a handy excuse not to do the chores.

I have counseled many teens who rationalize their irresponsibility to me by stating that the parents nag and yell at them "all the time" about doing something they've been asked to do.

In *Who's Raising Whom?* I discuss an interview with Steven, 15. Although I have not read of a description of this phenomenon anywhere, it has been brought to light by adolescents so many times in my office that I am certain that it is a part of the older child's developing psyche.

Steven's father told me that things had improved considerably around the house but that Steven had neglected to do the yard work last weekend. The father, as directed by me, had said nothing of it to his son.

Later, when I was alone with Steven, I asked him about the incomplete yard work. He replied, "Aw, Dad always bitches at me about the yard!"

I acknowledged to Steven that no one likes to be nagged at, but then I asked if Dad had nagged at him about the yard this last weekend. He thought for a second or two, then said, "No, but Dad *always* bitches at me about the yard!"

I then asked Steven if he was excusing himself (rationalizing) for not completing his current responsibilities because Dad had nagged him in the past. He smiled, shrugged his shoulders, and said, "I guess so."

Making Responsibility

Often I ask parents, when discussing their teen's responsibility, "What is our ultimate goal?" Most of the time parents realize that their long-term goal is to raise independent, responsible young adults. If this is the case—and I believe it is—what process do parents use to obtain this objective?

Parents often behave as if the way to create responsible young adults is to nag, remind, coerce, threaten, and punish them until they are 18 years old or so and then suddenly set them free—to be independent and responsible.

Children who are *made* to be responsible all their lives do not instantly become responsible the moment they leave the house and go to work or college. Instead, children who are *made* to act responsibly all their young lives will learn to become *dependent* on someone telling, reminding, and coercing them to be responsible. Like any complex behavior, responsibility must be learned over time. *Making* a child *become responsible* is a contradiction in terms and defeats the parents' purpose.

Every late May and early June, thousands of junior high school and high school graduates walk across their auditorium podiums and receive their diplomas. I believe that in many of these instances when the child's name is called the child should remain seated and his parents should walk across that stage. In probably hundreds, perhaps thousands, of cases it was the parent(s) who *made* that graduate do the homework and get organized—almost every weeknight of the school year. There are many thousands of parents out there who are earning a second high school degree.

The concern I have is, "What is the child learning?" Is the child learning to be a scholar? I don't believe so. I believe such children are learning how to become dependent on someone making them do their school work.

I firmly believe that by age 12 the pre-adolescent should be entirely accountable for his schoolwork. The parent is accountable for providing a desk or table, a chair, light, paper, and pencil, and for offering assistance when needed. But the child is accountable for the actual work.

The logical consequence for not doing homework is obvious—poor grades, repeating the grade, having to go to summer school or night school, or possibly even dropping out. I would prefer a child to earn C's on his own rather than earn A's because the parent was making him do so. In life, the independent C student might ultimately be more successful than the coerced A student.

I have seen many teens who repeated a grade return the next year with a new positive attitude. Moreover, I have worked with dozens of teens who dropped out of high school but, after flipping burgers for a few months, got their GED and went on to community college and did well.

The "school of hard knocks" can be an excellent teacher—far more effective than parental nagging.

A little-known statistic is that approximately one-third of college freshmen do not satisfactorily complete their first year of college and return for their sophomore year.

Why is that?

I believe a primary reason is that many of those young people were *made* to be responsible. Once they became college freshmen and were largely left on their own, they had not learned how to be independent and how to handle the time and freedom; therefore, they failed.

As I say to parents all the time, I would rather our kids fail now early in life than later—when the stakes are much higher.

Learning Responsibility

I often ask parents, "How did you learn to be responsible?"

Most of them say, "It happened over time." Most reasonable, responsible adults learn to be generally responsible through living awhile and experiencing logical consequences.

Mothers typically do not call their adult children and remind them it is time to go to work or to brush their teeth or to take out the garbage. Most adults simply learn that they can choose when to go to work, brush their teeth, or take out the garbage. At times adults might choose not to be responsible, but if they continue to choose such alternatives they quickly learn that they are unemployed, toothless, and living with rodents. Therefore, we ultimately learn to make reasonable choices.

How do we learn, for example, to operate and program a new VCR? We glance at the instructions and then we begin to fiddle with the buttons. In time, through trial and error, most of us (surely not all) learn to use the machine. The point here is that we learn by having specific instructions or a goal and by having sufficient time to experiment through our trials until we are successful and we progress and learn.

This is the model to use to teach our teens to be responsible:

1. Identify specific tasks and goals.
2. Give the teen the time and the opportunity to choose

to meet those goals.

3. Reinforce the teen for behaving responsibly.

4. If the teen chooses irresponsibly, ignore that poor behavior and allow the logical consequence to happen.

5. If deemed necessary, apply a specific consequence to the teen for a specific, seriously irresponsible behavior.

In this manner the parent no longer has the burden of *making* the teen behave responsibly; the parent simply identifies goals and rewards, ignores, or at times provides a consequence when the teen makes a bad behavior choice.

The parent is now off the hook. The parent is no longer the policeman.

The teen is "on the hook" to be responsible or not. Either way, the teen will learn—just the way most of us adults did.

When we over-police our kids to be responsible, we inadvertently teach them to be dependent on our coercion—and the pattern continues to spin.

In addition to fostering dependence, we might also be sending a poor message. The implicit message we send our kids when we over-direct (or over-protect) them is that we believe they are incompetent to make responsible choices on their own. When we allow our children to make their own choices, we send them the message that we assume they are sufficiently worthy and capable to generally make their own decisions.

Over-directing and over-protecting children and adolescents, then, lowers their sense of self-worth.

Responsibility Testing

If teens have lived in an environment where they have been *made* to be responsible most of their lives, they are likely to behave erratically for a time when the parents start allowing them to make choices about being responsible. Some teens will briefly take advantage of their new freedom. They might even try to force the parents back into the old role of "responsibility policemen."

Parents need to deep-breathe and hang in there, and in a relatively short time, hopefully, the teens will begin to "get with the program." Remember, even if the teens choose to be irresponsible, it can result in positive, therapeutic experiences.

Important Points To Remember in Chapter Four

1. Do not make the teen "even" after giving him or her a task to do.

2. *Making* a teen *be responsible* is a contradiction in terms.

3. Coercing responsible behavior only teaches dependence.

4. Over-directing teens lowers their sense of self-worth.

"The younger members of our society are not different from what they have always been. . .At the time of the world when there were only two young people, Cain and Abel, one of them was a delinquent."

Lord Aberdare

Chapter Five
Communication

In *Who's Raising Whom?* I placed little emphasis on communication. With children, I believe that it is more important what the parent *does* than what the parent *says.* Coping with adolescents, on the other hand, requires effective communication.

Effective communication occurs when both parties feel they have had an opportunity to express themselves and they feel they have been heard. Adolescents commonly complain that they "can't talk to" their parents who "don't understand."

Like any complex skill, effective communication requires learning and training; it does not come naturally.

Most parents commit one of more of the following sins of communication:

Monopolizing

When parents have conversations with their offspring, they typically do most—nearly all—of the talking. Some communication research has indicated that, when conversing with their children, parents monopolize upwards of 90 percent of the conversation.

A typical conversation consists of the parent making a point—at great length—interspersed with the parent asking the child a number of questions which are answered by a simple yes or no. Following the child's one-word response, the parent gallops on. Twenty minutes later the parent has rattled on for 19 minutes and 30 seconds and the child has spoken two "yes's," four "no's," and three "maybe's."

Is it any wonder that our kids often complain they "can't talk to" their parents and their parents "don't understand?"

To avoid monopolizing, parents must pay attention to the ratio of their speaking time to that of their child's. Effective communication assumes that the teen in the conversation will speak approximately one-half of the time—optimally even more so. The essence of effective communication with a teen is to have the teen express his or her feelings completely and appropriately.

The best way to facilitate communication with a teen is to frequently ask open-ended questions. Open-ended questions cannot be answered in a word or two and usually elicit a more extensive response. Common open-ended questions parents should frequently ask their teens are:

What do you think about. . .?

How do you feel about. . .?

What is your opinion about. . .?

In addition to open-ended questions, parents can encourage their teens to express themselves by saying things like "That's interesting" or "Tell me more about that."

Also, parents should establish and maintain eye contact, appear interested (even if they aren't), smile often, and *listen.*

Lecturing and Preaching

Lecturing and preaching are closely related to monopolizing in that the parent over-controls the conversation and does most, if not all, of the talking. The difference here is that, in addition to monopolizing the conversation, the parent takes on a moralistic tone and lectures, often at great length, to the teen.

More often than not, the teen has heard the lecture before—probably many times before. By the time our kids are five or six, they have probably heard every one of our speeches several times. With tongue in cheek, I have recommended on many occasions that parents number their speeches so that, when the need arises in the parents' minds to speechify, they can simply shout out the appropriate number and save their breath. That is about how effective their lectures are going to be anyhow.

When I was a teen and made my father angry (which didn't occur all that much!) he would lecture me for long periods of time. He would start each paragraph with "It's a fact!" and then ramble on, *ad nauseam*, it seemed to me. Once I heard the "It's a fact!" I would develop ear flaps and wouldn't really hear what he said. Besides, I had heard it all before.

When parents begin lecturing, and that tell-tale glaze comes over their adolescent's eyes, the parents are only listening to themselves. Parents lecture, I tend to believe, to reduce their own stress; it certainly doesn't educate their teens; nor does it facilitate communication with them.

Preaching is lecturing with morals. It often begins with the parent saying, "When I was your age. . ." and then the parent rambles on for 15 to 30 minutes. ("When I was your age I walked to school in the cold and the snow up-hill— both ways!")

Most teens believe that when their parents were young, dinosaurs walked the earth. I have had many adolescents argue that their parents were "born old." Moreover, as noted previously, adolescents tend to think their parents are dumb. Therefore, preaching is obviously not an effective way to teach values and deteriorates the communication process.

I have asked parents, "How much credence would you give a sermon if you thought the clergyman delivering the sermon was too old, not in touch with modern thinking, and was not at all interested in your point of view?" That's how our teens view our preaching.

Interrupting

In my work in marital and family therapy, I constantly see family members interrupt each other. One person begins a statement and suddenly another family member cuts in and begins talking. What typically results from this action is that the person being interrupted begins to speak louder, often to the point of shouting, and a short verbal battle ensues to determine who will control the conversation.

It is my professional experience that if a person (often the wife or the teen) is interrupted enough, that person will resign to the "one-down" position and will no longer try to participate in the dialogue (monologue?). Of course, that person also stops listening as well.

Be courteous; listen to your teen. Let your teen finish commenting and then state your position. By allowing your teen to speak fully, you will facilitate communication—and your teen will more likely *hear* you.

Dismissing or Talking Teens Out of Their Feelings

One way to teach teens that you can't communicate with them is to dismiss their feelings or try to talk them out of their feelings.

Steve, 15, says to his father, "I'm really scared about the basketball game, Dad." To which dad replies, "You don't have anything to worry about. It should be a snap. Stop being so scared. Don't be such a sissy. Besides, when I was your age. . ."

Sue, 16, says to her mom, "I'm so mad at Aunt Louise for what she said! I hate her!" Mom responds, "You don't mean that. Aunt Louise likes you. You're her favorite niece. I don't want to hear you talk like that any more!"

In these instances the parents dismissed the teens' feelings and argued that the teens shouldn't feel what they were, in fact, feeling. In each case the adolescent obviously was not being validated by the parent. Once again Steve and Sue learned that their parents do not listen, don't understand, and possibly do not even care.

Judging

A basic tenet of psychotherapy is that the therapist should not make value judgments about the client—especially about the client's feelings or attitudes. To a large degree parents should follow the same rule.

Tim, 17, reveals to his mother, "I was in the store and I was tempted to steal something. . .but I didn't." Mother replies, "That's terrible! You shouldn't even think that way. I'm not sure I can trust you to go out alone."

Scott, 17, shares with his father, "That Julie is really hot. I'm going to ask her out and take her to the drive-in." Dad responds, "What's wrong with you?! I can't believe a child of mine would think or say such a thing! I'm ashamed of you!"

These teens shared feelings and the parents immediately judged those feelings to be inappropriate. Parents are supposed to tell children if they believe their children's *behavior* is unacceptable. As our children grow older, we parents must be especially careful about making premature value judgments about their feelings, attitudes, or statements. We want to avoid teaching our teens that they cannot communicate with us.

Denying Perceptions

Early in my training, as I was being observed doing family therapy, a young mother once remarked to me early in a session that it seemed like it was getting cooler outside. I responded by saying something like, "I thought it actually has been sort of warm." At the end of the session, my supervising psychologist critiqued my session and said, "Never deny a patient's perception." He argued that once I suggested to the woman that I denied her view of the weather, she could not easily share any subsequent feelings with me. The same rule applies to parents.

If a teen happens to share a perception with a parent, the parent needs to avoid denying the teen's view or trying to correct it. All people, including our teens, are entitled to their own perceptions—right or wrong.

If parents want their teens to talk to them, they had better not deny their teens' perceptions when those perceptions are offered. Telling teens often that what they are thinking or feeling is wrong will definitely cause communications to stop and might also cause the teens to begin to doubt their own perceptions.

Facilitating Communication—Reflective Listening

Any psychologists worth their salt have learned reflective listening. Adolescents often respond well to me not because I am such a wonderful guy, but simply because I'm usually one of the first adult authority figures who appears to be genuinely interested in what they have to say.

Parents should not necessarily become their children's therapists. However, parents should develop some of the counseling techniques used by therapists to foster better communication with their teens.

With reflective listening, the parent commits none of the sins of communication. Instead, the reflective listener remains quiet, calm, and interested and virtually becomes a "mirror." Consider the following three examples:

Example No. 1
John, 14, is quite angry at being blamed by a teacher for something he feels he did not do: "Mrs. Fletcher is such a jerk! She always picks on me!"

Mom replies, "John, you seem upset. You feel Mrs. Fletcher is being unfair with you."

"That's right, Mom. Let me tell you what happened yesterday. . ."

Example No. 2

Kory, 15, is depressed over breaking up with her boy friend: "Mom, I loved him! What am I going to do?"

Mom says, "Kory, you really seem sad. Tell me more about it."

"Well," Kory replies, "we've been arguing for the past few weeks, but I didn't think it would lead to this. . ."

Example No. 3

James, 17, is making a "political" statement to his dad: "People are so stupid! If people can vote at 18, they should be allowed to drink. If you are old enough to die for our country you should be able to drink in it, too."

Dad responds, "You apparently have some strong feelings about this issue. Tell me more."

"Well, Dad, you know all the power in government is in the hands of the elderly people. . ."

In the three examples, the parents committed none of the sins of communication; instead, they listened, *paraphrased,* and often asked for more information. In all cases, the teens felt they were being heard, recognized that their parents understood, and were encouraged to continue expressing themselves.

In Example No. 1, most parents would typically have interrupted, monopolized, and lectured: "Hold it, John! Mrs. Fletcher doesn't pick on you for no reason. You must have done something wrong to make her angry. You are always causing trouble. How many times do I have to tell you to keep your trap shut?"

A typical parental reaction in Example No. 2: "Kory, what are you blabbering about? You were only dating him for a few months. You're so young. It was only puppy love. When I was your age I had dozens of break-ups. Wait till you're older. Then you'll know what real problems are." This response includes interpreting, interrupting, monopolizing, dismissing, preaching, and denying perceptions.

Example No. 3: "What the hell are you talking about? What do you know about politics! You and your half-baked ideas!" Classic use of interrupting and judging.

Communication as a Tool for Conflict Management

With a teen in the house, the scene is set for occasional (frequent?) arguments. By using effective communication techniques, the parents will not be able to prevent conflict but hopefully can resolve conflicts more easily and more quickly.

When Josh is upset about something and is angry with us, I try to sit calmly and fully elicit his point of view. When I do not interrupt and try to shout over him, the conflict level remains reasonable.

Once I believe I have Josh's complete perspective, I repeat it back to him. When he hears me paraphrase his argument, he can correct any of my misperceptions. At some point I will get Josh to admit that I have heard him accurately. Obviously, he cannot now complain that I did not listen or did not understand.

After obtaining acknowledgement from Josh that I heard his view, I will make my argument—calmly and precisely. I will highlight where we agree and disagree. In conclusion, I will make the final decision—sometimes pleasing Josh and sometimes not. In any event, the conflict level is minimized and Josh feels he was heard.

Let Me Get Back To You

Conflicts often occur when a teen wants permission to do one thing or another. The teen presses the parent for an immediate answer. Being uncertain, having little time, and being pressured, the parent naturally feels tense and often answers in the negative, largely because of being unable to consider a response and also because of being fearful of making a mistake by granting permission to do something inappropriate.

Sensing the parent's indecision, and being angry at the negative response, the teen badgers the parent to reconsider. Considerable arguing and conflict ensues.

When an adolescent requests permission for something or an answer that does not really require an immediate response, the parent should take some time, I believe. The parent should say something like, "This is important. I need some time to think about that. I will give you my answer this afternoon (or tomorrow)." In this manner, parents can consider the situation, discuss the issue with his spouse, and calmly make decisions without pressure.

Recently Josh asked me if he could attend an upcoming rock concert. After listening to his request I told him, "I'll get back to you on that tomorrow morning." I discussed the matter with Nan, and after a bit we agreed that we would prefer that Josh not go. The next morning Josh did not relish my response. But he knew I had pondered his request and came to a careful, considered decision. He complained briefly but let it be.

Parents United—Even If They Are Wrong

It is natural for people to have different points of view on various topics. Certainly this also applies to parents and the topic of raising their children. Parents should discuss their differences on child rearing in private—*not in front of the child.* A parent *must not* undermine or countermand the other parent in front of the teen. Such actions lead to badly behaved kids and a strained marriage.

A common pattern I see in my practice is one in which the mother feels Father is too harsh with the child, and Father feels Mother is too easy with the kid. To compensate for Dad's perceived strictness, Mother gives the kid more latitude than she normally would. To correct Mother's apparent laxity, Father tries to be even more restrictive with the child than he normally would be. The obvious result of this family situation is that the parents become increasingly polarized in their approach to the child, the child manipulates the parents to excess, and the marriage is seriously stressed.

This situation occurred when Josh was about eight or nine. It was Sunday morning, and Nan and I had had some words. She left the bedroom still upset with me. Several minutes later I overheard Nan and Josh arguing. A bit later, Josh approached me and said, "Dad, Mom is in one of her *moods.* All I did was say something, and she *over-reacted.* [Remember, he's lived with a psychologist his entire life—poor thing!] She told me I can't watch TV for the rest of the day. That's not fair! I want you to talk to her."

As I was listening to Josh, I thought he was correct. Nan was probably upset at me and vented some of that anger at Josh. Nevertheless, here is how I responded: "Josh, I do not appreciate you trying to get me to go against your mother. Therefore, not only will you not watch TV today, you're not going to watch it tomorrow as well!"

I believe that parents need to be united, in the eyes of the children, *even if they are wrong.* You do more damage by trying to correct the wrong by countering the other parent than by simply supporting the other parent—and discussing the situation later privately. Josh would live by going without TV for another day. It was more important for him to see that he could not manipulate us.

Of course, if one parent is being physically, emotionally, or sexually abusive to the child or teen, then the other parent must step in. Short of abuse, though, the parents should seem united even when one thinks the other parent is wrong.

Blended Families

Unity is especially necessary with blended families. In such families, kids are prone to argue that the step-parent "is not my real mother/father," and thus should not discipline them. In addition, children tend to complain to their natural parent that the step-parent is being unfair, thereby aligning with the natural parent against the step-parent.

I believe that if one cares enough for someone to live with, sleep with, and co-mingle funds with that person, then one should assume that that person will do a reasonable job of rearing the offspring of both parents.

Many people, it seems to me, make this implicit contract with their second (or third) spouse: "I love and honor you but I don't trust you enough to manage my kids." I think that attitude is foolish.

Splitting

A year or so ago I came to learn that Chad, then 11, had had a minor problem in school. Not wanting to disappoint me, he manipulated Nan into not telling me about the problem. When I subsequently learned of this, I argued to Nan that she allowed Chad to manipulate us—to *split* us, by forming this subtle alliance; in this case, of him and her against me.

We decided on a plan.

Several months later Chad had a minor problem at his after-school program. Again, when Nan picked him up, he tried to split us. Nan said nothing.

When Chad and Nan came home, Nan brought Chad to me and said (as planned), "Chad did not follow directions at PALS today *and* he tried to get me to not tell you!"

Chad was mortified and quickly learned to give up the "splitting."

Arguing Constructively

As already discussed at length, parents of teens cannot easily make them do something the teens do not choose to do. After parents have listened to their teens' perspective, reviewed the teens' points of view, and calmly presented their arguments, many teens will continue to push their points. At this juncture, I recommend that the parents calmly and distinctly restate their position on the matter. Then the parents should say something like, "You know how I feel about this issue. But I can't/won't make you do what I want. I have faith in you that you will do the right thing or come to the right decision."

In this manner, the parent clearly states a position but does not shove it down the teen's throat. The parent also implies faith in the teen to do the right thing. If the teen chooses correctly then the teen should be praised. If an incorrect choice or response is made, then logical consequences should generally be allowed to have their effect. In the case of the teen choosing very irresponsibly, punishment should be implemented.

Important Points To Remember in Chapter Five

1. When communicating with their teens, parents should avoid the sins of monopolizing, preaching, interrupting, dismissing, judging, and denying perceptions.

2. Parents should learn reflective listening techniques to facilitate communication with their teens and minimize the conflict level.

3. Parents must remain united in front of their children—even if they might be wrong.

4. Parents must not allow their children to split them. This admonition is especially important in blended families.

5. When in conflict with their teens, parents should state their position calmly and concisely. They should indicate that they cannot make them do what they want but that they have faith in the teens to do the right thing.

"A majority of young people seem to develop mental arteriosclerosis forty years before they get the physical kind."

Aldous Huxley

Chapter Six
Curfew and Money Matters

Curfew

In general, I view curfew as one of those walls parents set up that they have to defend. If your teens are going to misbehave, they can act out as easily before curfew as after.

Recently I asked a father why he was so set on maintaining an 11:00P.M. curfew for his 17-year-old daughter. After some hemming and hawing, he said, "Well, if she stays out too late only bad things can happen. She could get pregnant, you know!"

I wondered aloud to this father, "Could she conceive at 10:00P.M.?"

Probably the best explanation for a curfew that you can tell your teen is the following: "I love you and worry about you. I have difficulty going to sleep peacefully until you arrive safely home. Since I do not want to stay up all night worrying, I need you home by blank o'clock."

A general rule of thumb I suggest to most parents is to set their teen's curfew according to the curfew laws of the area. Since it is illegal for the teens to be out after curfew, they must be home by curfew time.

Another issue to share with your teens is that statistics indicate that most serious auto accidents occur after the bars close; thus, it would be prudent to be home well before that time.

Money Matters

Children will not begin to appreciate the value of a dollar until age 10 or 11 or so. When Josh was about 12 and Chad was about 7, my father-in-law used to enjoy occasionally giving his grandsons a silver dollar or a crisp dollar bill. Josh would greatly appreciate the gift—and often quickly spent it. Chad, emulating his older brother, would feign excitement but often I would later find his money left on the coffee table in the family room.

Adhering to my philosophy of letting teens learn from their mistakes, I believe that money management is learned only by being given the opportunity to handle one's own money. I find that parents typically dole out money to their older children as they need it; they coerce their teens to save money, yet give money to them when they want it—regardless of how the teens have handled money previously.

Once again, "the school of hard knocks" is probably the best teacher of money management.

Allowances

I've found that parents tend to deal with allowances arbitrarily. In some cases, if the kid is alive on Saturday the kid gets paid—regardless of performance and behavior the previous week. In other cases, the child might have been fairly responsible all week but failed to complete some task later in the week. The frustrated parent then yells, "OK, no allowance for you this week!"

I believe there should be a systematic relationship between the chores/jobs to be done and the amount of allowance given. Parents should clearly and specifically outline the chores—*what* is to be done, *how* it is to be done, and *when* it is to be done. A specific sum of money should be allotted to each task. If the task is done correctly, on time, the teen earns that amount toward that week's allowance.

I noted in *Who's Raising Whom?* that a family with whom I was working nearly blew several weeks of therapy due to a near-fight a teen had with his father. The teen was asked to wash the family truck—which he did. When the father realized his son had not wiped out the interior of the truck, they began to argue and nearly came to blows. Father later said to me, "Of course, everyone knows when washing a car/truck that you sweep the interior."

I was not so certain. Parents must be specific about the chore to be done.

As our children mature, we should give them increasing latitude about the time frame in which they do their tasks. Obviously, some chores must be done in a fairly narrow time frame, such as washing the dinner dishes and making beds. On the other hand, a broader time limit should be given to complete other tasks, such as "cut the grass on the weekend"; "wash the car sometime on Saturday"; "pull weeds on Sunday"; "clean your room before company comes."

Some parents over the years have told me they do not believe in giving their kids allowances. Their children should do their chores simply because they are part of the family. If children are doing what they are told to do and receiving money from the parents through some other system, fine.

Connecting specific chores to specific amounts, though, has been one of my most effective ways to encourage teens to complete their assigned chores. If teens are being generally responsible through some other system, then my method is not needed. "If it ain't broke, don't fix it."

If a parent uses a specific allowance system and the teen chooses not to do a certain chore, the parent should allow a sibling to do the task (if there is a sibling) for the allotted sum. If necessary, the parent can do the job and keep the money.

If the teen continues to omit a particular chore, increase the amount allocated to the task or add a bonus if all the chores are done. In this manner, if the teen chooses to be irresponsible, he gets hit where it hurts most—in the wallet.

Teens require quite a bit of money: spending money, school lunch money, transportation, lessons, school supplies, clothes, so forth. I recommend that parents sit down with their teen and calculate how much the teen will generally need each week for his expenses. The sum, then, becomes his allowance. It then becomes the teen's responsibility to manage that amount of money.

By adding all the necessary fees into the allowance system, parents often are able to apply considerable leverage in encouraging the teen to complete assigned chores. It is also interesting to watch teens as they initially struggle to juggle the money to meet all their needs. It is a great learning experience for them.

Brian, 15, required constant nagging to cut the grass (it took barely 30 minutes to do the job). After his parents set up the allowance system, Brian continued to need reminding. Getting tired of nagging, Brian's mother contacted the 14-year-old boy across the street and paid him the $4.50 to do the job. When Brian realized he was no longer going to be reminded to do his chore and the neighbor boy was going to get most of his allowance, he got with the program.

Money and Clothes

One of the most common arguments parents and teens have has to do with the teens' clothing. This is especially true with females. Wanting to be accepted by their peer group—as discussed earlier—teens often insist on purchasing only name-brand clothes that are terribly expensive.

I remember when Josh was about 13 he insisted that he wear only Guess jeans. We would go to the department store. A pair of Guess jeans would cost nearly $40.00. In the next bin was an array of generic jeans that looked nearly identical to the Guess jeans but cost only about $14.00. I tried to get across to Josh that he could buy nearly three pairs of the generic jeans for the price of one name-brand pair. I couldn't understand why a little tag on the back pocket was worth an extra $26.00.

Nan and I solved this problem early on. We agreed that Josh could update his wardrobe twice a year—for school in late August and during Easter break. Before each of these times, Nan and I would sit down with Josh and determine what his clothing needs were. We then decided on what was a reasonable amount to spend and than gave Josh the money to spend as he saw fit.

Not long after we began this program, I noticed that Josh was coming home with bags from discount stores and was becoming quite interested in sales. I recommend this practice highly. It saves a great deal of arguing and teaches the teen to manage his or her money more effectively.

Important Points To Remember in Chapter Six

1. Parents should explain why they are setting a curfew and should probably use the curfew laws of their neighborhood as their guide.

2. Allow teens to manage their own money so they can learn from their own mistakes and consider connecting chores with the allowance.

3. To avoid battles over clothes, decide on a reasonable clothing allowance and let the teen buy what he wants.

"As far as I am concerned, this book is an unauthorized biography!"

Josh Waldman

Chapter Seven
Getting Help

Stigma of Mental Health Care

Asked to speak to several hundred students at a local junior high school as part of a drug awareness program, I gave a 20-minute talk on "Drugs and the Family" that concluded with the following:

"Suppose, as you awaken one morning and step out of bed, you feel a sharp pain. You look down at your feet and you see that your big toe is all red, sore, and swollen, and it hurts to walk. How many of you would want to see a doctor?"

About three hundred hands shot up.

I continued, "Suppose you awaken one morning and you feel tired and blue. And you realize that this is not the first morning you've awakened this way; in fact, you've been feeling like this for the past few weeks. You feel sad and pessimistic. You lack your normal energy and have lost interest in doing things you used to enjoy doing. You have become more isolated and your friends say you are more irritable. You are not eating or sleeping well. You recognize that you are depressed. Although you have not mentioned it to anyone, you have begun to wonder what it might be like to hurt yourself. How many of you, then, would want to see a doctor?"

Barely a dozen hands went up.

I responded to the auditorium full of seventh, eighth, and ninth graders, "I guess you people care more about your big toe than you do about your mind!"

Their response was no surprise. By the time our children reach the age of 12, they have already learned the stigma of mental health care. In our society we have one set of beliefs about physical medical problems and quite a different set of beliefs about behavioral, emotional, and psychological ones.

If a person has a physical medical problem—a broken leg resulting from a fall, for example—we do not assume that he deserved that problem; we do not assume that the person caused the problem; we do not believe that such a person is bad because of that problem; we assume that the person needs help; we do not make that person feel ashamed because of that problem; we rush down to the hospital and draw pretty pictures on that person's cast and cheerfully provide encouragement.

We make just the opposite assumptions concerning behavioral, psychological, emotional problems. If a person becomes depressed, for example, we often assume that he caused the problem and perhaps deserves it; we make that person feel bad and inferior about emotional problems and cause him to feel shame; we tend to shy away from a person with psychological problems; we either discourage that person from seeking help or make the suggestion to "tough it out," "buck up," "pull yourself up by your bootstraps," or simply "get a good night's sleep."

I can't say how many times I have done an initial intake on a seriously disturbed child. I ask, "Why hasn't this child been seen previously?" The mother often replies, "Because his father has said, 'No kid of mine is ever going to see a shrink!'"

We tend to stick our heads in the sand when it comes to mental health issues. The same parents who run to the pediatrician every time their child coughs or has a runny nose will, despite the obvious need, procrastinate for years before they have their child seen by a mental health professional.

Where is it written that it is OK to get help from the neck down but it is not OK to seek help for the mind?

Without a doubt, the most common health problem in the United States involves mental, emotional illness. A recent lead article in *Newsweek* estimated that about 20 percent of the adult population presently suffers from a major psychiatric disorder—depression and anxiety being the most common. Nevertheless, people react to psychological problems as if they are some deep, dark, mystical, unusual, rare illness.

This stereotypical, short-sighted thinking prevents people from seeking the help they might need. One thing we know for certain in this business—the sooner one addresses psychological problems, the sooner and the easier they are to correct; the longer one allows emotional problems to continue, the more intractable they become.

I believe that if the family and the child or teen are essentially "normal," by using the ideas presented in my books most "normal" problems can be solved. However, if the family and child or teen have not resolved their problems despite intervention, the responsible parent, I submit, must seek help.

Warning Signs

When in trouble behaviorally, emotionally, or chemically, adolescents—unlike children—send warning signals that are similar to those of adults. A bench-mark of the mental status of adolescents is to examine their performance in all the basic arenas: home, school, peer group, and community.

Many teens have some problems in one area. If a teen has difficulties in more than one area—especially in all of the arenas—that teen most likely is in serious psychological difficulty and in need of professional help.

Here is a list of warning signs that suggest the teen is behaviorally, psychologically, or emotionally at risk:

1. Frequent breaking of *basic* family rules (defiance), including staying out all night and/or running away.

2. *Any* violence toward parents or verbal threats of harm and/or frequent aggression toward siblings.

3. Frequent serious emotional outbursts or temper tantrums, which might include destructive acts.

4. Increased periods of isolation in the teen's room. (Some isolation from their family by teens is normal—annoying, but normal.)

5. Any statement of self-destruction; for example: "I wish I were dead." "I wish I hadn't been born."

6. A significant change in the teen's sleeping behavior—sleeping excessively or barely sleeping at all.

7. A significant change in the teen's eating pattern—eating excessively or not being able to eat at all. For females, watch if they seem uncomfortable after eating and excuse themselves and immediately go to the bathroom (bulimia).

8. A significant change in energy level, where the teen appears especially lethargic; pay particular attention if the teen seems to give up activities that were previously enjoyed.

9. A sudden disinterest by the teen in hygiene and appearance.

10. Increased fears (such as of crowded public places, driving, or making a mistake) and tension, often accompanied by pacing and agitation.

11. Periods of depression followed by brief periods of hyperactivity or super excitement along with little sleeping or eating (pay particular attention if a history of manic-depression disorder exists in the family).

12. Any bizarre behavior, strange or illogical beliefs, or an awareness of stimuli that do not exist.

13. A significant drop in grades—not just B's to C's; teachers complaining that the teen is suddenly no longer completing assignments and is cutting class.

14. Cutting classes in school, frequent fights with other students, several confrontations with staff, numerous detentions and/or a suspension or expulsion.

15. The teen has no friends or apparently has lost his friends; a distinct change of friends; new peers seem more deviant and several of them have been known to have been in trouble.

16. Problems with authorities such as shoplifting, vandalism, burglary, and joyriding.

Problems with drugs with our teens, unfortunately, are quite prevalent. Research suggests that there might well be a gene that increases a person's predisposition to chemical dependency. If a grandparent or parent has or had a problem with drugs or alcohol, the odds for substance abuse and addiction in the teen increase dramatically (by better than 50 percent).

If chemical dependency is in the family, parents must be particularly attuned to the above list of warning signs. They must also be especially aware of the signs in their adolescents:

1. Erratic, unpredictable behavior and abrupt changes in mood.

2. Drunkenness; glassy, red eyes; silly, giggly, or hyperactive behavior.

3. Alcohol on breath; liquor or beer containers seen; the pungent smell of marijuana in the room or car or on clothes; and drug paraphernalia—matches, cigarette papers, small pipes, razor blades, pill vials, plastic baggies, so forth.

4. Disappearance from the house of money or items that can easily be sold, such as jewelry, cassette tapes or compact discs, and small electronic equipment items.

5. Acquisition by the teen of things he cannot afford—jewelry, tapes and discs, electronic equipment, leather jackets, premium sneakers, and so on.

6. Confirmation of the arrest for drug involvement of a peer who is a close friend of your teen.

7. Any arrest involving drugs; for example: DUI, minor possession, disturbing the peace. Never accept "I was just holding it [drug] for a friend"—that's the oldest dodge in the book.

8. Frequent, brief phone conversations between your teen and others—often late into the night; consistent hang-ups when you answer the phone; your teen leaving the house for brief periods of time for no apparent reason; frequent furtive meetings with your teen and someone else (who might be much younger or older than your adolescent) to whom your teen refuses to introduce you. (Such activity suggests the possibility of drug dealing.)

If your teen displays any of these signs, especially two or more, your teen might well be in trouble and should be offered help. As I once said in a workshop, "If we do not give assistance to our teens when they need it, our teens will ultimately get help—from a judge. . .or a mortician."

If you are not sure your teen requires professional help, see one anyhow. The worst that could happen is that a competent, ethical professional will set your mind at ease and tell you that your situation is normal.

Helping Professionals: M.A., M.Ed., M.C., M.S.W., D.S.W., Ph.D., Psy.D., M.D.

In addition to the these abbreviations, mental health professionals use the following titles: therapist, psychotherapist, clinician, counselor, social worker, clinical social worker, psychologist, clinical psychologist, counseling psychologist, psychiatrist, and biological psychiatrist—and I probably have omitted a few.

It is no wonder that the public is bewildered when it comes to mental health. Furthermore, the media often confuses psychology with psychiatry.

Generally, mental health professionals can be grouped into three categories:

1. Individuals with master's degrees,
2. Individuals with doctoral degrees, or
3. Individuals with medical degrees.

Professionals with master's degrees (M.S.W., M.S., M.Ed.) refer to themselves as clinical social workers, counselors, therapists, or psychotherapists. They usually have a graduate degree (typically requiring two or three years' study) in psychology, education, or social work. Often they are licensed by the state and—at the time of this writing—charge $50 to $90 an hour for their services, depending on the area. Their fees often are covered, in part, by the client's health insurance plan (typically under the Mental and Nervous Disorder provision of the plan).

Professionals with doctoral degrees (D.S.W., Ph.D., Psy.D.) refer to themselves as doctors of social work (D.S.W.) or of psychology. They possess graduate degrees (usually taking four to six years of study), sometimes in education or social work but usually in clinical psychology, educational psychology, or counseling psychology. They are usually licensed by the state and charge $80 to $120 per hour for their services, depending on their area. Their fees are usually covered, in part, by applicable insurance plans.

Professionals with medical degrees (M.D.) refer to themselves as psychiatrists or biological psychiatrists. They have a general medical degree (four years) and an internship and residency (total of about six years) during which they specialize in psychiatry. (However, I know of several family physicians who gave up their medical practices to see only patients with mental health issues.) Psychiatrists are licensed by the state and charge $90 to $175 per hour for their services, depending on the area. Their fees are usually covered, in part, by applicable health insurance plans.

Since psychiatrists are medically trained, they tend to see problems more from a biological perspective, while therapists with master's and doctoral degrees tend to view problems more from a psychological, environmental, or cognitive perspective. Only psychiatrists can prescribe medication.

It is not true that M.D.s are better than Ph.D.s who are better than M.A.s when it comes to providing family therapy. Some master's-level clinicians are outstanding therapists, and some psychiatrists do not do much psychotherapy. The primary issue, I believe, is how much experience the professional has had working with adolescents and their families. Since I chose to obtain a Ph.D., I obviously believe that a combination of extensive training and experience in this field is best.

I find it surprising that many people still do not realize that their health insurance plans not only cover them when they are sick with the flu but also cover mental health services. Psychological, behavioral, and possibly even educational problems with your teen might well be covered by your insurance plan. You are paying for the benefits; if you need them, use them.

If you have no funds or insurance plan, contact a reputable local mental health agency and seek treatment perhaps on a sliding-scale basis. Many social service agencies provide mental health treatment to individuals and families with fees based on the client's ability to pay; sometimes the fees are as little as $5 per session. For treatment in these situations, the client does not select the therapist; rather, it is the other way around. Therapists in these settings often are young and inexperienced, but they usually are supervised by an experienced social worker, psychologist, or psychiatrist.

Where To Look For Help

It is my experience that most people find their therapists through the Yellow Pages—as they would pick a plumber. Obviously, I do not recommend this practice.

The best method to locate a competent, experienced therapist is to contact the family doctor or child's pediatrician, assuming the teen is still being treated by one. Even if you are new in town, ask the doctor's receptionist to whom the doctor refers parents for problems with teens. Most family physicians and pediatricians maintain relationships with competent therapists with proven track records.

Another acceptable method is to contact a specialist at the teen's school: nurse, counselor, school psychologist, or principal. Usually these individuals have referral relationships with appropriate professionals.

Today, many families belong to HMOs or other managed-care health insurance plans. Parents can contact the intake or referral coordinator of their plan and ask for an appropriate referral to a professional in the program.

Finally, parents can contact the local Psychology Informational and Referral (I&R) number in the phone book and probably secure a good therapist. Generally, you can be certain that psychologists on the I&R service are competent and ethical.

Questions To Ask

When you first call the office of the therapist you have chosen or to whom you are referred, I recommend that you ask to speak directly to the professional, talking no more than five minutes, and ask the following questions:

1. Are you licensed or certified by the state?

2. How long have you been in practice?

3. How much experience have you had dealing with oppositional adolescents? (Be sure to give your child's age.)

4. What is your professional, theoretical orientation (behavioral, cognitive, biological, psychoanalytic, or eclectic)?

5. What are your fees and how is insurance handled?

6. Can you help me if medication or hospitalization is needed?

7. Do you want to see my child for the first session?

How To Be a Good Patient/Client

Psychotherapy is a two-part process: the therapist must conduct the treatment appropriately, and the patient must fulfill his role as well.

Patients should therefore adhere to the following:

1. Arrive on time and be prepared to leave at the designated end of the session.

2. Pay your bill promptly. Do not let money get in the way of the treatment.

3. Implement recommendations faithfully; do your homework!

4. Ask questions of the therapist if you are unsure of anything. If you are dissatisfied with something, discuss

it. If you can't discuss your misgivings with your therapist, who can you talk to?

5. If, after six sessions, things are not better and you have already discussed this matter with your therapist, find another one.

Coming In For Help

In my years of private practice, I have met only two teens who requested that they see a therapist. In the vast majority of cases, it is the parents who initiate the treatment.

Adolescents are usually reluctant to become involved in treatment for several reasons. Like many adults, they hold a misguided view of mental health and believe that to see a therapist means they are "crazy" or "bad." They believe the parents are the ones with the problems and that they should get help, not them. Finally, they assume the therapist will side with their parents against them.

Parents should try to counter these views before beginning treatment. They should point out that normally one sees a professional for a medical problem, so one should see a professional for a behavioral or psychological or family problem. Most importantly, the parents should stress that the *family* is coming in for treatment and that the teen is not being designated as the "bad patient." The parents should emphasize that they want to help the teen and also learn how they can more effectively communicate and live with the adolescent.

Any good, competent treatment concerning an adolescent should certainly involve the parents—and possibly the entire family.

If the adolescent refuses to participate in treatment (which is fairly common) or refuses to speak during a session (a common threat but rare in practice), the parent should come anyhow. I tell parents to tell their adolescents the following: "I'm going to see the therapist and we will be talking about you and making plans about you. We would like you to participate in that process. If you choose not to become involved, I can't make you, but we will go on without you."

Most teens usually choose to become involved. Even if the teen refuses to participate directly in the treatment, however, many parents have found considerable success seeking treatment themselves.

If the parent changes, the teen changes.

Progress in Mental Therapy

Parents often assume that progress in mental health issues takes the form of progress with medical issues. With most medical illnesses, the course of the illness is fairly well understood. With pneumonia, for example, by day five the patient has typical symptoms, which worsen by day ten, and so forth. Once treatment is begun, the patient exhibits certain characteristics by five, ten, and thirty days later—until the patient is free of the sickness.

Such is not the case with mental health problems. People do not get "sick" within a few days, and they typically are not "cured" twenty or thirty days after treatment has been initiated. The path of mental health progress is uneven.

Suppose someone decided to go on a diet to lose 25 pounds and we charted their weight every morning at the same time for 90 days. What would the graph look like? A straight line descending down over the course of the ninety days (assuming the diet was successful)?

No. The line would be a jagged, up-and-down one, with progress followed by regression, followed by progress. If the diet ultimately was successful, the final point of the line would be lower than the starting point, but the path from the beginning to the end would certainly be uneven.

This is the course of progress in mental health. Parents often get discouraged when, after working with me a bit, they see some improvement in their teen, only to see some of the old problems reoccur. Some parents feel as though "we're back to square one."

Obviously, this is not the case. Progress is made unevenly—two steps forward and one step back. As we've discussed, therapeutic events can result from inappropriate behavior.

Just like the dieter who overeats during a meal or two, one cannot give up; the dieter and the parent must continue with the program as consistently as possible.

Tough Love

Within the past decade, in many communities a self-help program has developed for parents with problems with their rebellious teens. This program is known as Tough Love. It was begun by David and Phyllis York in Pennsylvania as a result of problems they incurred with their adolescent daughter. Tough Love branches can be found in every major city.

I agree with much of the philosophy of Tough Love. However, in my experience, I have seen parents who become involved in Tough Love before they ever receive any professional help. I believe this is a mistake.

Parents with a problematic teen should first consult a professional. If treatment has been attempted and the teen remains uncooperative and irresponsible, then seeking the support and guidance of a Tough Love support group is, I believe, warranted.

Hospitalization

Much has recently been written about hospitalizing adolescents unnecessarily. There apparently has been some abuse of this tactic. However, let's not throw the baby out with the bath water.

My basic approach to coping with adolescents is based

on the premise that the teens ultimately will come to learn to behave responsibly due to the consequences the parents consistently provide following the teens' behavior. This approach assumes that the teens are capable of learning and are not dangers to themselves or to others while they are reflecting on the consequences of their acts.

If a teen's thinking is clouded by excessive drugs or alcohol or the insidious influence of a gang, cult, or physical or sexual abuse, that adolescent is out of control and cannot learn effectively. Moreover, if the teen is engaging in destructive behavior to himself or herself or to others, the teen must be protected and controlled. In such situations, hospitalization is in order.

Most communities have adolescent treatment centers. I have seen many teens who were completely out of control go on to do quite well following a short stay (15 to 45 days) in an in-patient adolescent facility.

If a teen is out of control, particularly if out-patient counseling has been tried, hospitalization must be considered. Contact your mental health professional or a local adolescent treatment facility for more information.

Good luck.

Important Points To Remember in Chapter Seven

1. We make opposite but incorrect assumptions regarding problems of physical health versus problems of mental health.

2. If problems with a teen persist, the responsible parent seeks professional help.

3. Parents should be aware of the warning signs of a teen in trouble.

4. To find a qualified, appropriate professional, call your family physician, pediatrician, selected school staff, intake office of your HMO, or local I&R service.

5. Parents should ask questions of their family therapist and be good patients.

6. If a teen refuses to participate in treatment, the parents can still benefit from counseling without him.

BIBLIOGRAPHY

Bayard, R.T., and J. Bayard. *How to Deal With Your Acting Up Teenager*. New York: M. Evans and Company, 1981.

Buntmān, P.H., and E.M. Saris. *How to Live With Your Teenager: A Survivor's Handbook for Parents*. Pasadena, CA: Birch Tree Press, 1979.

Dinkmeyer, D., and G.D. McKay. *Systematic Training for Effective Parenting of Teens*. Circle Pines, MN: American Guidance Service, 1990.

Ginott, H. *Between Parent and Teenager*. Toronto: Macmillan Company, 1969.

Gordon, T. *Parent Effectiveness Training*. New York: Peter M. Ogden, 1970.

King, P. *Sex, Drugs, and Rock and Roll: Healing Today's Troubled Youth*. Bellevue, WA: Professional Counselor Books, 1990.

Robin, A.L., and S.L. Foster. *Negotiating Parent-Adolescent Conflict*. New York: Guilford Press, 1989.

York, P., D. York, and T. Wachtel. *Toughlove Solutions*. New York: Bantam Books, 1984.

About the Author

The success of *Who's Raising Whom? A Parent's Guide to Effective Child Discipline*, Dr. Larry Waldman's first book, led him to do this sequel. Dr. Waldman received his B.S. degree in psychology and his M.S. degree in educational psychology from University of Wisconsin; his Ph.D. degree in educational psychology was from Arizona State University. He has been a teacher at high school, junior college, and university levels; a school counselor; a school psychologist; a consultant; a psychologist affiliated with a hospital; and a clinical psychologist in private practice. He has served as a part-time member of the staff at Arizona State University since 1977 as professor in the Department of Special Education. He has counseled thousands of children, teens, and parents. A resident of Phoenix, Arizona, Dr. Waldman is an accomplished public speaker and lectures nationally.

Hampton Roads publishes a variety of books on metaphysical, spiritual, health-related, and general interest subjects. Would you like to be notified as we publish new books in your area of interest? If you would like a copy of our latest catalog, just call toll-free, (800) 766-8009, or send your name and address to:

Hampton Roads Publishing Company, Inc.
891 Norfolk Square
Norfolk, VA 23502